Published by The Blackberry Preserve
Montgomery, AL and Houston, TX
www.theblackberrypreserve.com

Designer: Frederick James Pellum III, of
Passion Energy Lighthouse, LLC
Illustrator: Faroah Sharp
Consultants: Jaylin Brown & William Brown IV
Page 4 photo courtesy: Dr. Elizabeth Dawson, Director and Archivist of the Meek-Eaton Southeastern Regional Black
Archives Research Center and Museum
Page 37 photo courtesy: Jabari Cain of CainsCamera.com
ISBN-13: 978-0692494844
ISBN-10: 0692494847

THIS BELONGS TO SUPERHERO

As a man thinketh in his heart, so is he. -ancient proverb

A NOTE FROM A SUPERHERO:

Throughout time, the African-American male has achieved greatness in many disciplines and areas of required knowledge. They have done so despite both obvious and unseen challenges. Dr. Kimberly Brown has captured the essence of this in her treatise, *Superhero Like Me*. In too many instances, however, traditional narratives omit this information and record of accomplishment. So much damage is done to young people, especially to their conceptualization of the world and self-identity, when they grow up deficient of healthy and affirming images. This literary work could not come at a better time. These pages and powerful illustrations function as a useful reference for our children as they prepare to create a better future for humankind.

I encourage both youth and parent readers to allow the stories captured within to guide you toward your own superpowers and the motivation to use them to change the world. Let's begin now with *Superhero Like Me*.

Dr. Frederick S. Humphries,
President Emeritus of Tennessee State University
and the illustrious Florida Agricultural & Mechanical University

Do you know about Ramses the Great who ruled Egypt as Pharaoh?
He was a warrior-king who defeated his rivals with giant chariots, bows and arrows!

His army had one hundred thousand men and he built many cities for all to view.
Nine other kings used his name, but none of them could do it quite like Ramses 2.

He ruled the whole empire for more than 60 years, you see.
Yeah, that's right. He's a real life superhero

...like me!

Then there was Mansa Musa, the richest man of all time!
He controlled the Kingdom of Mali,
which had so much gold the whole world could see it shine.

He took his royal court, horses and camels on a super trip across the land.
The way he gave away his treasures along the route was like a parade, so grand!

He built an awesome school in Timbuktu, you see.
Yeah, that's right. He's a real life superhero

...like me!

Shhhh… Listen…

Toussaint was one of the greatest military leaders the world has ever known!

France became rich from all the sugar their slaves had grown.

Toussaint was super smart. He read a lot and knew this wasn't right.

He led his people to fight for freedom with all of their might.

France kidnapped Toussaint, but they didn't know he had a buddy named Jean (John)

who kept leading the battle until the slaves had won!

They were so proud of what Toussaint started, they put his face on money, you see.

Yeah, that's right. He's a real life superhero

…like me!

Frederick Douglass came on through to help people too.
His magical hair gave him superpowers to do something terrific every time it grew!

He wrote his own books and newspapers and traveled around the world.
He taught that cheating and bullying was wrong, and that boys should respect girls.

He believed in always being fair and asked,
"What to the slave is the 4th of July?" you see.
Yeah, that's right. He's a real life superhero

…like me!

Wow! Booker T. Washington was an amazing kid
who used thinking as his super tool.
He'd do a day's work before daylight,
then change the clocks just to make it on time to school!

His hard work and special chameleon powers made him the Great Wizard of Tuskegee.
Raising money and training students to build their own buildings always kept him busy.

He even made time for dinner with President Theodore Roosevelt, you see.
Yeah, that's right. He's a real life superhero

…like me!

Carter G. Woodson holds the special secret key to the past.
He wrote zillions of books so people could get all of the facts.

He chose February as a special time for everybody
to show what they learned during the year.
He treated the neighborhood kids to ice cream
and they would always cheer.

He lived in his office so he could afford to do this super important work, you see.
Yeah, that's right. He's a real life superhero

...like me!

The plant whisperer George Washington Carver
came to teach at Booker's school.
He was an expert in science
and so were Ernest Just and Dr. Charles Drew.

Daniel Hale Williams ran his own hospital
and put a man's broken heart back together again!
John Kevin Tucker healed kidneys
and Levi Watkins gave countless hearts a second wind.

Percy Julian invented medicines to get rid of people's pain and fix their eyes.
Dr. Lonnie Johnson studied at Tuskegee and made robots that help NASA astronauts fly.

Kids everywhere have a blast because Dr. Johnson invented the super soaker, you see.
Yeah, that's right. They're real life superheroes

…like me!

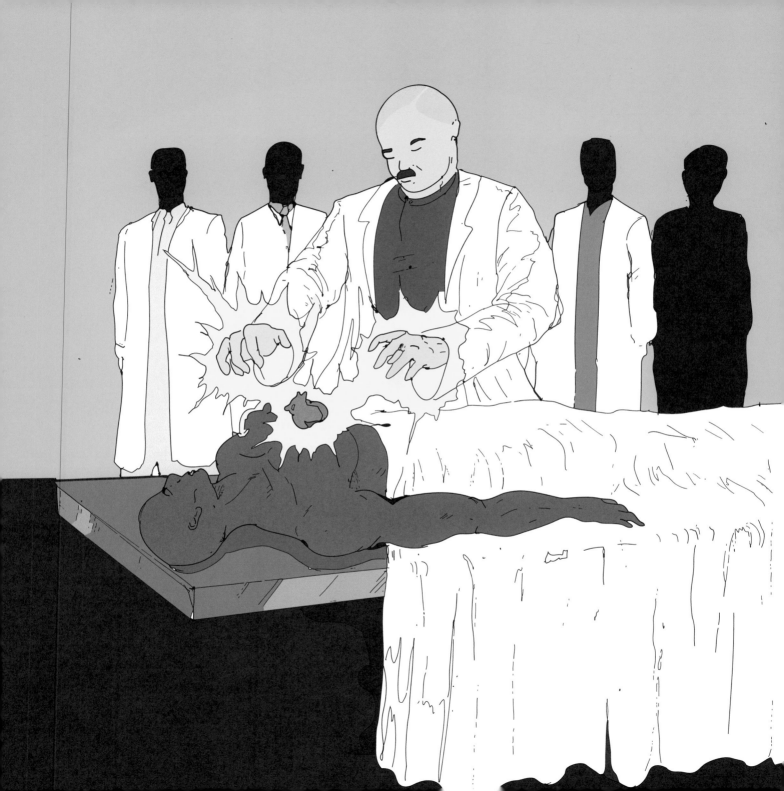

There is no one on earth who could throw a ball like Satchel Paige.
People would come from far and wide just to see him play.

But be sure, nobody can ever run as fast
as Cool Papa Bell.
He'd turn off the lights and be in bed before the room got dark.
That's the story Satchel liked to tell.

Josh Gibson was a power-hitter and a fantastic catcher too.
Homerun king! How could he knock that ball so far? The people didn't have a clue.

They all played together in their own super league, you see.
Yeah, that's right. They're real life superheroes

…like me!

Can you believe people told the Tuskegee Airmen they couldn't fly?
But a lady hero named Mary McLeod Bethune dared to ask, "Why?"

Despite the big bullies,
they became navigators, pilots and super champions of the air!
They trained hard and performed with such precision,
they helped the U.S. military become more fair.

Benjamin O. Davis, Jr. and the Red Tails got special medals
for aviation in World War 2, you see.
Yeah, that's right. They're real life superheroes

...like me!

Dr. Martin Luther King is known all around the world for his super special dream.
He got his superpowers to lead a mass movement because of a super special team.

Medgar Evars, E.D. Nixon and Fred Shuttlesworth sacrificed
to make sure all people are treated the same.
It's important to read, study and speak at our very best, just like Malcolm X,
so their work won't be in vain.

They have colleges, monuments and whole airports named after them, you see!
Yeah, that's right. They're real life superheroes

…like me!

Jake Gaither was a super rattler
who coached a winning football team for 25 years!
He took his FAMU athletes to play the University of Tampa
with absolutely no fear.

It was the first time a game like that happened in the South
and FAMU won 34 to 28!
And don't forget before Walter Payton was an NFL running back,
he played like a tiger at Jackson State.

Legend Eddie Robinson won 408 games
and had a Super Bowl dedicated to him, you see.
Yeah, that's right. They're real life superheroes

…like me!

Some heroes have special musical powers
that transform people when they sing.
The way B.B. King plucked his guitar, Lucille,
made her sound like she had magical strings!

Stevie Wonder can close his eyes and see music
in a place that no one else can grasp.
James Brown could do splits in the air!
Louis, Miles and Dizzy breathed cool life into jazz.

MJ walked on the moon
and had socks so glittery they were visible from space, you see.
Yeah, that's right. They're real life superheroes

…like me!

Did you know TuPac Amaru Shakur
was named after an Incan king?
Just like Langston Hughes,
he became one of the greatest poets the world has ever seen.

He studied at a school named after Paul Lawrence Dunbar,
who was a famous poet too.
TuPac was a fine actor and learned Shakespeare
because reading was one of his favorite things to do.

His library was filled to the sky with books of all kinds.
This is how so many words filled up his brilliant mind.

He taught us to keep our heads up and love our dear mamas, you see.
Yeah, that's right. He's a real life superhero

…like me.

Now I'm super cool! I feel like a king when my barber edges up my hair.
I'm sitting on my throne ready to rule my empire when I rest in his chair.

He's my personal magician.
The way he uses his clippers is so precise.
When I take off my royal cape,
I'm ready for the world because he's got me looking just right.

He is smart and fun, and he's his own boss, you see.
Yeah, that's right. He's a real life superhero

…like me.

When I look in the mirror I know I am the best.

Thinking about who I am makes me stick out my chest.

I can run. I can jump. And I can flex my muscles too.

I can do math and every day I read so much I get ideas that are brand spanking new!

It's in my DNA! I can look at champions all around me,

just as easy as I can count to three.

Yeah that's right. You can try, but nobody else can be a SUPER DUPER HERO

… like me!

MY FAVORITE SUPERHEROES:

_____

_____

_____

_____

_____

_____

About The Author:

"Limits on our potential evaporate when we can look in the mirror and like what we SEE."

Dr. Kimberly Brown earned a doctoral degree in United States history at Howard University and has worked as a Goldman Sachs Multicultural Fellow at the Smithsonian Institution National Museum of American History.

In 2015, the Smithsonian-Anacostia Museum library chose *Queen Like Me: The True Story of Girls who Changed the World*, Dr. Brown's history book for girls, as their newest acquisition for its children's literature collection and the Southeastern Region of Jack and Jill of America, Inc. recognized it in its official reading recommendations for youth. Since authoring the book, Dr.Brown has partnered with museums, libraries and youth-related organizations throughout the country as a keynote speaker and workshop facilitator. She has served the United Negro College Fund as moderator and panelist for its nationwide "Empower Me Tour," which seeks to effectively equip high school students for success in college.

Currently, Dr. Brown teaches at Texas Southern University. She applies her specialization as a scholar to assist youth with minimizing the influence of imposed standards and negative stereotypes, but rather cultivating positive self-identities for themselves and travels extensively to fulfill this mission. The Meek-Eaton Black Archives Research Center, in Tallahassee, Florida, has installed a collection of women's history archival materials named in Dr. Brown's honor.

Dr. Kimberly Brown often shares, "Limits on our potential evaporate when we can look in the mirror and like what we see."

Dr. Kimberly Brown is pictured above with Creative Consultants Jaylin Brown and William Brown IV.
Visit www.EducationLikeMe.com for complimentary learning resources.

Made in United States
Troutdale, OR
03/06/2024

18174518R00024